BAD.BOYS.MOM.

by
Jasmine Lequay Arrick

TABLE OF CONTENTS

INTRODUCTION 5

CHAPTER 1 15

CHAPTER 2 21

CHAPTER 3 33

CHAPTER 4 41

CHAPTER 5 51

CHAPTER 6 55

CHAPTER 7 59

CHAPTER 8 63

CHAPTER 9 69

CHAPTER 10 79

CONCLUSION 87

VISION BOARD 91

LETTER TO ELLIE WITH LOVE 95

Copyright © 2020 J. Elle LLC

www.jasminelequay.com

INTRODUCTION

WHO DO YOU THINK YOU ARE?

Do you think everything you've been through in your childhood, good and bad, especially the bad, truly affects the kind of parent you are or will become? I believe it does—but it doesn't always have to. Our childhood experiences are often reflected in our adult lives, but we must remember that we are always in control of ourselves and can make the choice of exactly who we want to be, how we want to think, and how we want to live our own lives at any point in time.

I've noticed that, in life, most of us seem to only embrace the blissful moments, and we so deeply fear the struggle and everything that comes with it. Throughout my life of living and learning, I have chosen to embrace the highs and the lows. I have learned that all of the struggles and negativity we as women may experience can actually uplift us, guide us, and strengthen us. There is so much value, even in our struggles. If you can positively shift your perspective, you will be able to find the value in most situations.

I'm sharing my thoughts, my experiences, my business tactics, and the daily routines that have helped me to evolve as a person and, most importantly, as a parent. It took me some time, but I have learned that self-love is the key to happiness in every area of our lives. I have discovered that there are ways to still love yourself, even when others couldn't. I will introduce you to specific practices you can exercise to increase that self-love in your own life right now.

Over the years, as I've lived in a few different major cities and met women from different backgrounds and lifestyles, I have noticed that even though we may be very different, we all want relatively the same things. We all want love, loyalty, and respect, and sadly we all quite often have similar stories of heartbreak, abuse, and some life experiences we are even ashamed of. I think most of us have been through things that we have kept to ourselves, things that may have broken us down for some time, but we chose to remain resilient. In those resilient moments, we show ourselves what we are truly capable of. That is the beauty of the pain.

Resilient: To be strong and to keep pushing forward towards your goals. To get back up after every fall knowing your purpose is much bigger than any defeat!

In this life, we are presented with blessings and lessons. And as great as the blessings are, the hard lessons are what usually give us character. We should embrace those hard life lessons and use them as learning experiences. My journey of a single pregnancy, and being a single mother has taught me so much about myself. I went through many hard lessons, and I've been shown strength in myself that I never knew I had. If someone would have asked me before any of this occurred, if I thought I could have survived these difficult circumstances and come out better than before, I would have answered, "there's no way possible." I couldn't have imagined that I would be living this single mom's life and eventually turning myself into a successful and strong Bad.Boss.Mom.

At times, I have been lost, heartbroken, abused, misled, and misunderstood. During my lowest points, I made some of the best self-improvement decisions of my life. There may be days that try to break down every part of you that you are trying so hard to keep put together. I know that feeling. I know the feeling of having very little support, yet being required to carry the weight of the world on your shoulders. And on the brighter side, I also know the feeling of winning in the face of opposition, of beating the odds, and of truly being internally happy despite adverse circumstances in life. Through a journey of self-care, self-love, and a spiritual connection with God, I believe we can overcome it all. We can conquer anything!

Those goals and dreams you thought you'd have to give up on because you became a mother can be brought back to life. You can balance it all. You can live a life of fulfillment mentally, physically, and spiritually. You can attract to yourself the relationships you want, and the career and the life that you deserve even as a mother. Even as a single mother if that's your reality! All you need is a lot of perseverance, a positive mind, a grateful heart, and a solid plan of action.

Ladies, this is our story. The story of the resilient woman. It is still being written and far from over—this is truly only the beginning. Let's be thankful for the adventure and take a look back at how far we have come. Let's live to make our own lives a testimony of positive growth for others and especially for our children. Let's shed that cocoon and grow into the most beautiful butterflies. Let's forget about everything negative we once thought about ourselves and become the women we've always dreamed to be.

I am currently on my own Bad.Boss.Mom. Journey and I believe that every woman will eventually reach hers, in her own way.

No two paths are meant to be the same. Yours will be a unique reflection of what God has planned for you in God's perfect timing for your life. A Bad.Boss.Mom. is someone who is a role model and a leader for others, someone who makes a way and provides for her family no matter what. She also provides others around her with opportunities to grow and better themselves. She is someone who is a positive force in this world, and she is making positive impacts in more lives than just her's. She is someone who rises back up with a mind of optimism after she has been knocked down. Her true beauty is shown throughout her actions and love for others. She inspires other women, supports other women, and uplifts other women. She does not back down, and she does not let fear get in her way! It is time to get into alignment with your goals and become the Bad.Boss.Mom. that you are destined to be.

I can Manifest whatever I want! – note to self

BAD.BOSS.MOM ANTHEM

I can't be stopped; I'm reaching for the top,
You can come, too, but here's what you must do.
Promise to love yourself, promise to do your best,
Be the best mom you can be and always let love lead,
Don't take shit from anyone, Boss Up and get it done,
A Bad.Boss.Mom. is who you're destined to be,
Keeping pushing through those obstacles,
Accepting no defeat!

I am Jasmine Lequay Arrick. I am a 28-year-old single mother of one, a business owner, a Realtor, a serial entrepreneur, and now so proud to be an author. My accomplishments did not come easily or overnight. Those who know me personally in life have likely seen that I've been through my fair share of "hell" before reaching some "glory," and I am nowhere near where I intend to be. I'm only here telling my story now because I haven't let that "hell" stop me from my goals. I keep fighting, and I keep pushing forward.

My daughter's name is J'elle Imani, or Ellie as I like to call her, and she is one-and-a-half years old. I believe the true purpose of my existence was to be her mother and to lead her. She has the most vibrant energy and kindest little personality. She spends the majority of her time, either laughing and smiling or giving me many reasons to do the same. I look right at her, and I know that she is extremely special and that she will be such a strong and positive person in this world. I know that raising her right and watching her succeed in this life will be by far my greatest accomplishment.

Although motherhood comes with its many struggles, it is surely the biggest blessing any woman could ever receive. Even though I am fairly new to motherhood, I feel I have plenty to share that could be very helpful to other women, whether she is planning for pregnancy in the future, currently expecting, or already a mother.

It hasn't been easy, but I've been very fortunate to be able to maintain and balance it all pretty well as a single mother. I keep

God first always. I thoroughly believe in the laws of attraction and manifestation. I believe positive thoughts lead to positive outcomes. I practice daily self-care habits that keep my energy and my mind in a high vibrational frequency. This is so important because, after all, everything starts as a thought from the mind. I believe it is so critical to your internal happiness to keep a peaceful mind. It is also critical that you disregard negative thoughts as they arise in your mind. As soon as you receive one, refocus your attention on something you are very grateful for. I also like to say to myself, "God, release me from this or I rebuke this negativity," and it then truly feels like a weight has been lifted off me. I do this several times throughout the day, as much as needed. We all know how those fear-driven thoughts like to creep up on us and consume our mental peace. This is a major yet extremely simple practice that I recommend.

I have also discovered that you must choose happiness, as cliche as it may sound. Happiness is truly a choice. You will not just finally reach a point in your life one day where you stop and say, "okay, I can be happy now." No, you must choose to be happy even on the "bad days," even when it seems as if the devil is trying you.

Although it isn't realistic to believe we will always be happy at all times, we can always be grateful instead. Because if you are living and breathing, there is always at least one thing to be grateful for, and being in a state of gratitude often leads to you feeling "happy."

As I grow older every year and learn more about myself and life, I have realized that happiness is truly not a destination; it is a journey. Enjoy it all. The ups, the downs, the bumps, the bruises, and the victories! I can't wait to share with you how I am navigating through my journey.

CHAPTER 1

HOW A DYSFUNCTIONAL UPBRINGING CAN AFFECT YOUR PARENTING

Our upbringings and life experiences are constantly molding us. What we learn or go through in childhood is likely to affect us throughout our lives. We may notice that we are passing morals and beliefs from these experiences down to our children, but we often outgrow these old ways, and it's never too late to make changes for the better. Recognizing that you are evolving as a person and that there are adjustments that need to be made is such a beautiful headspace to be in. It is the true recognition of your mental growth.

If like me, you grew up as the oldest with multiple younger siblings who you looked after quite often, it may feel like you've always been a parent. At least, in my case, it did. Being the oldest has always put a lot of pressure on me. I've always known that I have so many looking up to me, and I've always wanted to make them proud. I also wanted to make sure they didn't have to learn things the hard way, as I had to in many situations.

A couple of my siblings have been through a lot in their lives. Three of my siblings and I share the same mother, and three other siblings share the same father with me. My oldest brother and I are the only two who share both the same mother and father. My three siblings on my dad's side were raised with their moms, and unfortunately, often grew up with very unstable circumstances. This has always been extremely upsetting to me but has motivated me more than anything to go harder so that I can help provide for them financially as well as be a positive role model in their lives. I have learned that what breaks me down in life and make me upset are the same things that encourage me to Boss Up!

Boss Up: Get on your shit, get your shit together, reach your goals, become more financially successful, and spread the wealth and knowledge to the ones you care for.

I am the product of a teen mother. My mother was sixteen years old when she gave birth to me, and my brother was born a year later. She and my dad separated very shortly after she had my brother due to my dad's bad drug addictions at that time. Understandably my mother wasn't quite ready to take on the extreme responsibility of raising children as a teen all by herself. So she allowed my grandparents to take over full custody of my brother and I. We lived with and were raised by them for close to twelve years. Most of my childhood, my grandparents did not have the most stable environment, either.

They were pretty young themselves at the time, right around the age of forty, they did a lot of partying and still wanted to live their own lives but also loved us very much and wanted to help my mom. My childhood growing up with my grandparents was quite dysfunctional, but it was also filled with a lot of loving and joyful moments. I never felt a lack of love in their home, and I am very thankful for that.

While living with my grandparents, I would often visit and spend weekends with my mom, but I always felt emotionally distant from her. I didn't necessarily know how to express this to her at such a young age. Even though there was a disconnect in our relationship, I was still always happy and eager to see her. She was so young and beautiful, and I truly admired her and still do till this day. It's funny to think back and remember how I would take pictures of her with me to school and keep them in my backpack to show her off to my friends, who were wowed by her beauty too. I adored her, but I just simply couldn't understand why I wasn't able to live with her at that time. I have many great memories of my childhood visits to my mother's home. I loved helping her take care of my younger sister, Deisha, she born when I was five years old. I loved to help feed her, bathe her, and change her. These tasks were a big responsibility for me at the age of five, but I really enjoyed it. I've always been the kind of person who loved to help in any way possible, even as a young child.

Sometimes those visits to my mother's home took a turn for the worse. My brother and I would witness my mother being abused by Deisha's dad. He would lock my brother and I in the closet sometimes while he abused my mother, and two times I can remember breaking free and running to the neighbors' home for them to call the police to help us. This caused a lot of emotional trauma in my life back then. I can still remember the fear that shot through my body as I heard her scream and cry for help and the anger that I felt burning inside of me because there wasn't much I could do to get him off her. I would imagine running up to this demon of a man and jumping on his back and pulling him to the ground so that my brother and I could hurt him just like he was hurting my mom.

I can still hear the pounding of my heart, feel the sweat dripping down my forehead, and the tears falling down my cheeks as I clenched my fists and bit my lips to keep from screaming at the top of my lungs as I waited for it all to be over with. This went on for a couple of years off and on. My mom would lie to my grandparents about cuts and bruises on her body, but my brother and I could always recall the abuse that we saw and heard and share it with them.

On a couple of occasions, my grandfather even got into physical altercations with Deisha's dad while trying to get my mom away from him. I was always so scared that one day my grandmother would have to tell me that he had seriously hurt my mom or, even worse, killed her. Worrying about this gave me terrible anxiety as a child.

Even today, it angers me so deeply to see any kind of abuse being done to others. I am always compelled to stand up for the victim in these situations. I believe it comes from the feeling of not being able to stand up for my mom back then when I felt so little and insignificant. I was so happy when my mom finally gained the strength to leave Deisha's dad for good.

After years of visiting my mom, my brother and I officially went to live with her after my grandpa died in a car accident when I was eleven years old. This took a major toll on us because our grandfather had raised us and had been like a dad to us our entire childhood. I have so many great memories of him and his loving and goofy personality. I also have a tattoo on my right shoulder in his memory, and there truly isn't a day that passes when he doesn't cross my mind. I like to think he's very proud of me and the woman I've become. That thought warms my heart, and I believe that I am being guided by him, and all of my lost loved ones.

As if losing him wasn't hard enough, a major transition took place in my life the day after his funeral. My grandma picked up my brother and I's belongings, and we left to live with our mom from that moment on. I was just a preteen at this time, grieving heavily and trying to build a relationship with my mother that we didn't really have before. I was dealing with a lot mentally at that young age, and it was causing me to act out at home.

Middle school was rough for me too. My grades were always good—I was usually a straight-A student—but I had extreme social anxiety. We moved around quite often, and it seemed like I was going to a new school every single year. I felt lost and disconnected. It was hard for me to make friends because of the constant moving. This was only the beginning of what would turn out to be a pretty rough teenage experience with many lessons learned the hard way.

CHAPTER 2

WHEN HISTORY REPEATS ITSELF

Seeing my mother being abused for years by my sister's father surely impacted my view on what the relationship dynamic between a woman and a man should look like. I also ended up in a very abusive relationship, in my first ever relationship at the age of sixteen. It was almost as if history was repeating itself. I stayed in this abusive relationship for a little over two years. My boyfriend, at the time, was two years older than me. He was involved "in the street life." He grew up around it, and statistics prove that we do tend to become products of our environments, and it is up to us to change the narrative of our own lives.

Most of his older cousins were dealing drugs or in prison at the time. He was a very negative influence on me as a teenager. I was introduced to a life with him that truly was a reflection of many things that my mother had been through around that same age. One of the craziest memories of many that I have from these times is stopping by his grandmother's house to visit him very early on what seemed to be a normal morning.

As we hung out on his grandmother's living room couch watching TV, we heard an extremely loud BOOM come from the front door. It was one of the loudest noises I've ever heard in such close proximity. We both jumped up off the couch, not sure what was going on at that moment. His grandmother quickly ran out of her room, yelling, "What the hell is that?" Everyone looked around at each other with the same startled facial expressions. I thought maybe it was a robbery, but quickly learned a SWAT team had forced its way into the home. Officers rushed in with their extremely large guns drawn and told everyone to lay on the floor, face down.

As I lay on that floor in disbelief, my face planted in a very foul-smelling old section of carpet, I thought to myself; *I can't believe this is actually happening.* One week prior, during a no-knock raid in the same neighborhood, a young, innocent mother was shot and killed by the police with her baby in her arms. That incident was running through my mind, and I was very afraid of what this could turn into, so I made sure to follow every demand the SWAT team shouted at us. It seemed like this went on forever. In reality, it lasted for a little less than an hour. They pretty much destroyed his grandmother's home searching for drugs, money, and weapons. I couldn't believe they would treat her belongings, everything she'd worked so hard for her whole life, with such disrespect.

They were looking for my boyfriend's cousin, who apparently was on the run from the police at the time. They antagonized and interrogated all five of the adults in the house to get an answer to the cousin's whereabouts and arrested one of his other cousins who also had a warrant.

After they left, we all thanked God that no one had been seriously harmed. Most people would have taken this terrifying experience as a red flag or a sign to keep their distance from certain people or situations. Sadly, I had to experience quite a few crazy and drastic occurrences before it became clear to me that these were not the kinds of people I should involve myself with or the path I should be going down.

Things became worse and worse before I realized that my livelihood was truly in jeopardy in this relationship. The abuse worsened. It seemed like every other week, I had either a black eye or a busted lip, and one time it got as bad as him busting my head open during an argument after a guy from school called my cell phone. He snapped my phone in half and then proceeded to punch me in the face. I remember going blank and waking up seconds later with blood gushing out of my forehead. When he realized what he had done to me, he immediately began to plead, beg, cry, and apologize. The result of this incident was twenty stitches in my forehead. I still have a scar from it, and it is a constant reminder of my abusive past.

I made many excuses for him at the time because he had a very unfortunate upbringing. He grew up without his father, and his mother was a drug addict. He was raised by his grandma, too, and he had a lot of dysfunction in his life as I did. We were able to relate to each other in that way. I would feel so sorry for him that, regardless of how badly he was treating me, I would always find myself making excuses for him. I would take him back time and time again and lie to my friends about these constant bruises and black eyes that he had given me. I would usually say I got into a fight with a girl in my neighborhood or something of that nature.

I broke up with him for the last time right before my eighteenth birthday, when I learned that he had gotten a girl from my high school pregnant. These days I can just be thankful it was her and not me—I definitely dodged that bullet. When I told him it was over, he begged and pleaded for me to come to have one last conversation with him, and he promised he would keep his temper under control.

Unfortunately, that was a lie, and I fell in a terrible trap. He almost took my life that day. He beat me so badly that both of my eyes were almost swollen completely shut and drove me around in his car with a gun to my head, repeatedly telling me that he was going to kill me. I felt like that helpless and scared little girl again, locked away in the closet while my mother was beaten so many years ago. I saw that his rage had no limits, and I believed that he would truly kill me. He took my cell phone to be sure I couldn't make a call for help, and he continued to hit me as he drove around our small hometown of Lima, Ohio, with me in a headlock.

I begged and pleaded, telling him I couldn't breathe. I began to have a panic attack, but this didn't phase him. He would only lower the gun when there was another car in sight or when we approached a stoplight. After about an hour of driving around and antagonizing me, he decided to stop at a gas station. I guess he thought I would be too frightened to make a run for it. As soon as he got out to pump the gas, I flung open the squeaky old door of that Chevy and ran as fast as I could into that gas station, faster than I had ever run before, begging for help and for the clerk to call 911. I quickly ran behind the counter with the clerk, my heart pounding, and my mind racing with the fear that he would just come in and shoot me right there in front of everyone.

The clerk called the police immediately, telling me to get down under the counter where my boyfriend wouldn't be able to see me. It was too late, and he knew exactly where I went. He came inside, walked up to the clerk's counter, and shouted at me to come on before he pulled me from behind that counter. The clerk came to my defense and was not backing down. He urged him to leave and told him the police were on their way. After a brief moment of yelling at me to get my ass up and come with him, he ran out of the gas station, jumped in his car and took off in a hurry. I'm sure everyone nearby heard the loud screech of his tires as he burnt rubber speeding off.

Shortly after, the police arrived, and it was all over. He was eventually arrested, and I promised myself from that day forward that I would never allow anyone to treat me that way again. I promised I would close that chapter of my life for good. I knew I was so young, with so much life and potential ahead of me, and it would all be wasted if I didn't smarten up right then and there and choose better for myself. I'm still so thankful that I survived that day. I can remember being extremely angry at that point in my life that I didn't have a father figure around to stand up for me or to protect me from situations like that and many others that I had gone through.

It became very evident that history had repeated itself. What I had witnessed my mother go through, I had become a victim of myself. This goes to show exactly why it is so important and critical that children aren't exposed to these kinds of situations. Childhood is the most fragile time as a human, and it must be handled with so much love and care.

We have so many adults in this world dealing with mental health issues because of things they have seen or been through in their childhoods, and it is time we break that cycle with our children. Let's raise children who don't have to recover from their childhoods, and who can be fully equipped for this world because of the way we've raised them. Children who will love themselves and love others.

My relationship with my mother grew a lot during my later teen years because I began to mature and understand her. I let go of the resentment that I had felt from my childhood. I was able to understand why she made the decision, as a teen, to give us to our grandparents, and I knew it was truly only for the best. I eventually understood that it wasn't because she didn't love me; it was because she loved me just that much. She wanted so much better for me than she could offer at that moment.

We particularly became closer when she gave birth to my youngest sister, Damia. I was turning seventeen at that time. I helped my mom a lot when Damia was a baby because she was a hard-working mother, and it was only right that I help take some weight off her shoulders in any way I could. Mom was working third shift at her nursing job, so Damia would often sleep with me, and I helped with her throughout the day too. Damia's father was present, but he also worked a full-time job and wasn't in the home often. Damia and I became very close, and we still are. It almost felt like Damia was mine sometimes because of our extremely close bond.

Helping take care of her taught me a lot about caring for an infant, and watching my mom balance it all taught me a lot about the "full-time working mom struggles." I was able to see firsthand how essential every aspect of caring for a baby is, from their sleep schedule to their feeding schedule to their nighttime routine and learning activities, etc. I was able to be a major part of my baby sister's growth and development, and I learned so many fundamentals about childcare and motherhood this way. That learning experience as a teenager definitely plays a role in the mother I am today.

Before I left home at eighteen, I gained so much respect for my mother. Her strength, especially, was something I was able to admire. She went from struggling as a single teen mom and having to allow my brother and I to be raised by our grandparents to, now, a hardworking and independent nurse doing pretty well for herself. I grew to understand more and more how giving us to our grandparents was a painful sacrifice, but a necessary one to allow her to get her own life together over the years.

She went back to school, earned her degree, and completely left behind her abusive past. Recognizing that the same strength had been instilled in me was such a beautiful realization. When I say my mom worked hard as a nurse, I mean it. My mother worked hard to ensure that we did not lack anything. She provided for us on her own, and she had truly reached her stage of being a Bad.Boss.Mom. I'm quite sure I'm able to be a Bad.Boss.Mom. because I saw her do it first.

My mother has always been quite a private and guarded person, and she doesn't often talk about the things that she has been through, but she sat me down one day and told me she had been molested as a child. I immediately began to hug her and cry. It was so heartbreaking to hear her story. I knew this may have directly affected her views on her self-worth and may have played a part in why she was so accepting of bad and abusive relationships throughout her young adult life. I wanted to just be there for her at that moment, but I also needed to share with her that I had also experienced sexual abuse at the age of thirteen. Besides my mother, I haven't shared this with many.

I am sharing this here because I have survived this experience, left it in my past, and have successfully moved on with my life. I want any woman reading this who has experienced any kind of abuse to know that it does not have to define you. You are not your past. You don't have to live in fear or shame of this. It isn't your fault. There is so much more to you than what has happened to you. You can rise above it all and still be proud of who you are and what you have made it through. I hope I can be an inspiration for that strength. You must let go of everything negative that you are holding on to. Releasing that shame from my mind was what helped me the most.

As women, we go through so much and are so often misunderstood. Sometimes this may lead you to ask yourself, is all of this struggle and pain truly worth it? I know I have. The moment I held my daughter in my arms in that hospital room, it all began to make sense. She was worth everything. She was my purpose in making it through it all. I went through close to twenty hours of excruciating pain while in labor. I screamed, I cried, I laughed, and I experienced love and fear, all while awaiting her arrival.

Her oxygen rate, as well as mine, dropped during labor, and I was placed on a breathing machine with our vital signs being closely monitored. I began to have an anxiety attack and became so worried that I wouldn't be able to deliver her safely. To make matters worse, when it was time to push, I tried my hardest, but she was stuck in my birth canal. After thirty minutes of reaching inside me and trying to reposition her for safe delivery, my doctor decided that we must do an emergency C-section.

At this point, I was in so much pain and so anxious to safely give birth to and meet my daughter that I was pleased to hear a C-section would be the solution. Thankfully during my pregnancy, I had done some of my research on C-sections just in case, so I was pretty well informed, and I felt very comfortable with the procedure. I was given an epidural and rushed to a different room for the C-section delivery. Twenty minutes later, my doctor said, "Okay, you're going to feel a lot of pressure." Boy, I did feel the pressure, it felt just like the doctor said it would, as if an elephant had rested its foot on my chest. It was very uncomfortable, but not painful. A few moments went by, and I then heard my baby's sweet little cry, and I began to cry, too. Her dad said to me, "She's so beautiful. She looks just like her sisters," referring to his other two children.

I was so excited to see and hold her, even though my body felt very weak and was shaking from the meds and the procedure. I was so ready to love and kiss my baby girl. This was the most beautiful moment I have ever experienced in my life. In that very instant, I realized that all of the hurt, the neglect, and the abuse I had been through in my life actually had a greater purpose. I now had my little piece of heaven that I could love, cherish, respect, uplift, guide, and teach. I vowed that I would protect her and pray over her daily, and God willing, keep her safe always from every kind of hurt. I will love her unconditionally for eternity. I thanked God for my daughter at that moment, and I have ever since.

Be the woman
you want your
daughter to be

CHAPTER 3

GETTING THROUGH PREGNANCY ALONE + SELF-CARE TIPS

There are so many amazingly strong and independent single mothers out there, and we really need to pat ourselves on the back. It's not easy, but we do it all so gracefully, so efficiently, and with so much resilience! I began this single mom journey at just five months pregnant with Ellie. I made the brave and bold decision to remove myself from a relationship with her father that had suddenly taken a turn for the worse. It quickly turned from a fairytale into a nightmare. That chapter is all very much behind me now, just a piece of my story and I am thankful for that.

The removal of that relationship from my life was a huge blessing in disguise. I don't believe there is any battle without some sort of God-given glory. Spending my pregnancy alone and struggling with that fact—and everything else that comes with pregnancy, including the ups and downs of hormones—actually brought me out on the other side a million times stronger and one hell of a woman! It brought me closer to God, and it showed me that self-love and self-care are much more important than any amount of love any man can give to you.

Just like those heartbreaks and struggles in my childhood made me stronger, this time during my pregnancy made me that much stronger too. One of my favorite sayings is that there's always some light in any darkness—that's the God in it. There is always a light at the end of a dark tunnel, ladies; you must keep pushing forward!

I can't even express the extreme importance of taking care of YOU first! As women, we are the root of all. We are where everything begins. We must nurture ourselves so that everything else can grow fruitfully. Our children don't need perfect mothers, just happy ones!

I began my self-care journey kind of by default. I was by myself and in my apartment alone most of the time during my pregnancy—because, I mean, what else is there to do when you're pregnant? Unfortunately, most of your "friends" are too busy for the prego chick. Although I have a one really great friend that I met in LA, Joselyn, and she was the best support system and cuddle buddy throughout my pregnancy. She would bring me food, escort me to OB appointments, and also join me for plenty of movie nights. When she wasn't around, I would either be studying or practicing my self-care.

I began to focus on reading more books—self-help, in particular, books about positivity, the law of attraction, and financial literacy. I wanted to increase my understanding in all of these areas. I hoped to become an all-around better version of myself through reading and exercising what I had learned. Some of my favorite books that I read during my pregnancy were *The Four Agreements, The Law of Attraction, The Secret, How to Meditate, Rich Dad, Poor Dad, and The Awakened Family*. I highly recommend all of these. I learned from The Law of Attraction that literally anything is possible. Nothing in this world is off-limits.

Your desires can be delivered to you if you can focus on them and put in the work to obtain them. The law of attraction can be described as an invisible force all around us. Just as powerful, if not more powerful than electricity, it is affecting us all, whether we believe it or not. Our own thoughts and beliefs guide the law of attraction. What we say, think, and believe is being attracted to us at all times. We can attract positives and negatives to ourselves, and that is why it is so important to think positively as much as possible.

I also began practicing meditation and daily prayer. I listened to the *Positive Head* podcast every morning. I returned to the church and connecting myself with God more than ever before. I fell in love with the woman that I was becoming. I loved that, even though I had some really down moments and often felt alone, I was usually able to snap right out of that and refocus my attention to a state of gratitude. Practicing daily gratitude and waking up each morning and writing down five things I was grateful for was something I learned from reading *The Secret* and, man, was this simple task so powerful!

Outside of everything I was doing for self-care, I always had this burning desire and motivation to stay productive. So, I decided I wanted to focus my time on becoming a true Bad.Boss. Mom., even before my daughter was due to arrive. I knew I wanted to be my own boss and make my own schedule so that I could have as much time as possible to spend with Ellie. So I launched my online clothing boutique, J.elle Collection. I love everything about fashion, and I really loved being a creative director and designer. I absolutely loved styling the models that I hired for my photoshoots in LA. Making others look and feel their best has been a passion of mine since I was a child. I adored playing dress-up. I loved picking out my friends' clothes and styling them from head to toe, even at seven years old. Finding your passion in life is very important. I have two tips on how to stay motivated, productive, and most importantly, happy during your pregnancy and how to use that time to find your passion.

Tip 1: Start a self-care routine

Come up with a daily routine that is not so much a task but actions that you are taking to make yourself feel good, to unwind, and to relax. This should be all about you! I recommend prayer, meditation, positivity journaling, working on a vision board, relaxing in a bubble bath while reading a book, doing a breathing exercise, doing yoga or another workout regimen, taking a walk in nature, and writing positive reminders on your bathroom or bedroom mirror to look at daily as a constant reminder of your uniqueness, beauty, and strength.

All of these tasks are life-changing, as simple as they may seem. They are so impactful on your vibrational frequency. While pregnant and single and refocusing my attention to positivity, I came up with the idea to start my self-care routine. I knew I needed to love myself and take care of myself so I could take care of everything else properly. My self-care routine was a complete game-changer for me. I found so much peace and was able to connect with my higher self through these activities. I still practice these routines today. I also recommend finding a strong support system during your pregnancy. Unfortunately, I did not have any family living in LA, and that's where I spent the majority of my pregnancy, but if you are blessed to be living near close friends and family, utilize that support!

TIP 2: Find a career or a hobby you are passionate about

I have learned from experience that staying busy and doing something you love, whether you are being paid for it or not, really keeps you in a happy state of mind. Find your passion! If you don't know what it is that you are truly passionate about, make a list of hobbies that you would enjoy doing and that you could do for countless hours with very little or no pay. If you are willing to do something for free, it usually means that your heart is in it more than your mind, and I believe that passion comes from the heart. Think back to things that you enjoyed doing as a child and see if you can incorporate them somehow into your adult life.

List 10 things that you are grateful for:

_____

_____

_____

_____

_____

_____

_____

_____

_____

_____

_____

_____

_____

_____

_____

_____

_____

_____

_____

_____

Remember to be grateful for everything that you have, while aligning with everything that you want!

Today is the
opportunity to build
the future you want

CHAPTER 4

HOW I STARTED MY BUSINESSES WHILE PREGNANT AND AS A NEW MOM

Always use your current circumstances as motivation. Especially if you are bringing a child into this world, make that your motivation to do more, to do better, and to become your best self! Remember, there are literally women out here who have multiple children and who don't have much help, who work more than one job, and sometimes who even go to school on top of it all, and they are still reaching their goals. We cannot get comfortable with making excuses for ourselves. When we decide to believe in ourselves and our strength, our power is limitless.

I began working on my own clothing designs before meeting Ellie's father and becoming pregnant with her. I visited a friend in London, U.K., for six months and began working with a seamstress on my designs and samples. I created six sample designs in London and planned a trip to Santorini, Greece, shortly after for business as well as my 26th birthday. I flew to Santorini from London, and my mother and Deisha met me there. I used that vacay to enhance my brand and get some amazing photos in my clothing designs for my social media and my website.

Santorini was a dream and by far, one of my top favorite places that I've ever visited—and I am pretty well-traveled. The photoshoot was a success. My younger sister Deisha turned out to be quite the photographer, and I was so excited after my trip. I couldn't wait to get back home to LA to find a manufacturer to get my samples produced and start planning for my clothing boutique launch, but things didn't go quite as I planned. I began dating Ellie's father shortly after I returned home to LA. Everything moved pretty quickly. He moved me to Philadelphia to live with him, and I soon noticed that I had become distracted. I began to focus more on my relationship while my goals with my clothing designs and boutique were taking a backseat. I think, as women, we often do this when in a new and fun relationship.

A couple of months passed by, and we found out that I was pregnant. At the time, her father was much more excited than I. I didn't feel like I was ready or had enough accomplished at the time. I had finally gotten so close to my goals, and I knew that having a baby could potentially slow me down. I became a bit discouraged. Her father reassured me that he would be there for us and have my back every step of the way. Those feelings of worry and fear soon began to disappear, and I put my energy back into my goals. I also knew that I needed to have multiple streams of income in place for the security of my child's future, so back to work it was! Her father was very supportive of this dream of mine at the time, and we began to put energy and money into making sure my boutique would be successful.

When our relationship didn't work out, and I decided to move back home to LA, I was still very focused on my goals, and I told myself that I wouldn't let all of the negativity going on between us stop me. Although I was very motivated, I did experience a lot of frustrations and setbacks. It was not at all easy being new to a business that I didn't know much about while in the middle of my pregnancy. I lost a lot of money because I didn't have much guidance on what I was doing. I hired a company to do my website for my clothing boutique, and they basically scammed me for close to $3K. I then had to hire another website design company.

After taking my time and doing proper research, I found an amazing company, Dlynthebrand. They completed my site quickly and exactly how I had imagined it to be. I began to work with a clothing manufacturer that I had paid close to $15K, and I am still going through a legal process with this horrible company. I'm hoping to be rewarded those funds back, due to the company producing very low-quality items way outside of our deadline dates, and behaving very unprofessionally. They also "lost" the initial sample designs that I provided to them.

As you can see, I took a lot of losses before reaping any reward, and still haven't seen much reward from this business investment. Even though it has cost me time and money, I wouldn't do anything differently if I could do it all again. I learned a lot from those losses. Every time I took an "L," it forced me to find the right way to get it done or showed me another way around it. Every setback is an opportunity to learn and grow.

"L": A loss, but in my opinion, a loss is never truly a loss. It's an experience to learn from a mistake and become better.

After going through such a hard time with manufacturing my designs, I decided to try a different route. I began to explore the world of wholesale fashion, which I noticed was working well for other boutique owners. I lived near the LA fashion district, and this was the perfect place to find wholesale vendors for my clothing boutique. I started to buy large quantities of different items that I loved, and I believed my target market would love too.

I initially planned to be the main model for my brand, but I didn't expect to be close to six months pregnant when I was finally moving forward and ready to launch everything! So my sister Deisha was very happy to take on the role of being the face of my brand and the main model in my photoshoots. I needed more models than just my sister, so I began reaching out and hiring models from Instagram and planning photoshoots. Everything was finally coming together. And because I was planning to move back to Atlanta from LA, I really needed to move fast and take advantage of all of the resources LA had to offer in regards to my clothing boutique.

I launched my boutique, and I was thankful to see so much support and many purchases being made. It was doing well, but not as well as I had anticipated, and I became anxious to secure yet another stream of income. I've always had a lot of interest in real estate. Three years prior, I had written a goal down in my journal to get my Realtor's license and also to learn how to invest in and flip real estate. My brother Keith had been speaking to me for years about the value of owning assets and owning real estate. I have always admired his intelligence and have always wanted to make him proud. Even though he's a year younger than me, he leads me in so many ways. I knew he would be proud to see me get my license and invest in properties. I researched and found a good online course for Georgia so that I could get my license before moving back.

Six weeks before making my move to Atlanta, I enrolled with the Georgia MLS Real Estate Training Institute for the six-month online course. The online course was extremely hard for me because I am such a hands-on learner. I really prefer a classroom type of environment. Although it was difficult, I remained focused and dedicated most of my time to studying and learning. After all, most worthwhile things in life don't come easily. My clothing boutique, J.elle Collection, became a secondary priority for me at this time as I shifted my focus to real estate. I promised myself that I would come back to my boutique at a later date.

I started studying so hard every day that I rarely left my apartment unless it was to go to church or an OB appointment. I was moving through my online course pretty quickly and passing each chapter exam. I began my move to Atlanta and continued to work and study up until I completed my course. Ellie was just about two months old at this time.

After finishing the online course, it was time to take the exit exam and the state board exam. The exit exam had to be taken in person. I arrived at the testing site and eagerly took my exam. I felt pretty confident that I would pass, but I was so upset to get the news that I had failed my course exit exam on that first try. We were given two chances to pass before we would have to re-take the entire real estate course. I couldn't run the risk of failing again, so I immediately hired a tutor from Tutor.com. I studied with the tutor twice before going back the second time around to take my course exit exam.

Thankfully, I did pass that second time. I then had to prepare for the Georgia state board exam to actually become licensed. I definitely had so much anxiety about the state exam because I had many people tell me that they had failed it at least two to three times before passing. I could not afford to fail—I needed to succeed for my daughter. I wanted to pass the first time and be done with it so that I could begin working as an agent immediately. I manifested my goal to pass by writing my intentions down in my journal daily, studying extremely hard, and putting myself in alignment with only positive thoughts. I was either mommying or studying, and there wasn't time for much else. Thankfully it all paid off, and I successfully passed my state board exam on the first attempt. I was ecstatic! I interviewed with different brokerages and began networking to find a great mentor.

Even after becoming a licensed Realtor, I still didn't feel like I had found my absolute passion in life, so I took a look at my goals written down in my journal once again. For years, I have dreamed of opening a beauty bar that will offer an array of salon services, and I plan to incorporate my clothing boutique into it, as well. I want it to be a one-stop-shop for all women, and I have dreamed of designing the interior to perfection.

I have seen other women open beauty salons that were not very successful, and I believe it is because the owners themselves didn't actually have experience in the beauty field or have a solid clientele base. I didn't want to make this same mistake, and I knew I would need to get into the industry and learn a beauty trade, perfect it, and take the time to build up clientele first. I decided I would learn the eyelash extension application. I have always loved getting my own lashes done. I also knew that doing eyelashes could be a great way to network with women in Atlanta since I was once again new to the area. I was hoping to meet women who could become lifelong clients, who could support my beauty spa once it opened and who could even hire me to be their Realtor.

I knew this was an extremely necessary step to take before I could properly fulfill this dream of opening a successful beauty bar. I took an eight-hour training class to become certified as an eyelash extension tech and began to practice constantly in my free time. I became really good at this skill within six weeks, and I then began accepting clients. I created a lash room on the first floor of my townhome, and I scanned my clients carefully to be sure of who I was allowing to come to my home—especially for the safety of my newborn child.

My sister Deisha was helping me with Ellie up until I hired my first nanny. When my sister wasn't available, I would set up Ellie's swing in my lash room, and she would be right next to me as I worked. That swing was an absolute lifesaver! I worked from my home for about two months. I wanted to move to a salon suite as a second step toward my end goal, but I had to think smart. I did not want to add overhead expenses to my already extensive list of bills, especially being a single mother. I needed to be very smart and business-minded with all of my decisions. I waited another month to gain more revolving clients, and I then moved my business to a salon suite.

As my business became more and more popular, I had many women on Instagram, asking me if I taught lash-training classes myself. So I began to do some research and see how I could make this possible. I took some time out and created a lash course curriculum that I could teach my students and help get them certified. I began to offer traveling courses, as well. I have taught in Miami, LA, New York, Washington, DC, Philadelphia, and Ohio.

In 2019, my first year in business, I successfully and efficiently taught over thirty five women with my eyelash extension course. I quickly grew my business to six figures in that short period. I also have close to 25 revolving lash clients, and I'm feeling more secure than ever about my expansion plans and dreams of opening a full-service beauty bar.

When deciding that you want to have your own business, it's essential to do your due diligence, meaning that do the necessary research in whatever field you are interested in conquering. It is also helpful to begin to study people who have already been successful in those professions and who already have successful businesses. There aren't too many things that haven't been done already, so use others' success as a blueprint for you to reach your own goals. I love watching women take over and kick ass! There are so many successful young women out here right now. Never be afraid to reach out to them via social media or in person. You might just come across someone who was once in your shoes and doesn't mind dropping a few gems on you.

Never look for handouts, though. Most successful people that I know did it with very little help, and you can't expect someone who has worked hard to be where they are to just give you the entire recipe for nothing. You should always have something to bring to the table in return for helpful information. Supporting one another is a must. We have to help build each other up, ladies.

Just a girl with goals

CHAPTER 5

MOMS DON'T HAVE TO BE PERFECT, JUST BE HAPPY

It's so crazy how having a child can completely change you for the better in such a quick and short period. I have always been a highly motivated person and a go-getter, but throughout my early twenties, I would definitely say that I was more focused on enjoying life than I was on the "bigger picture." I was traveling to different countries at least a couple of times a year, I was dating, and I moved to a few major cities for new experiences.

Don't get me wrong, I wouldn't change much about how I was living, but I definitely wish my mindset would have been a bit more stable and wired to go after all my goals back then. I'm sure that I would have been much further along right now, with much more accomplished had I been more disciplined and had I known about the true power of the law of attraction and manifestation. But as the saying goes, you live, and you learn. I am thankful for every experience in my life, good and bad because they have shaped me and given me a unique character of my own. That's the beautiful thing about life; no two people live the same one. You can be whoever you want to be in this life, and as long as you are confident in that person you have decided to be, others will believe in that person too.

Before becoming a mother, I also didn't understand just how much of a challenge it can be to balance everything. I had an idea from watching my mom balance it all, but I didn't fully understand. So many of us make it look so easy, and I now know firsthand that it isn't. When you see a mother whose children are well put-together, whose home is in order, and who also looks damn good, applaud her because keeping it all together and balancing everything is tough! As mothers, we also tend to put ourselves last. We tend to be the most selfless of all people. There's so much beauty in our selfless nature, but we must never put our mental health last. We need to be sure to take out some time for ourselves every day.

If you are like me and want to continue to travel, enjoy life, and still have a social life as a mom, you must find balance. I know many moms deal with feeling guilty about taking time out for themselves, hanging out with friends, going on date nights, or just going out in general. I have experienced this myself, and it's truly not often that I am away from my child if it's not for business purposes so that I can provide for her. Even when I do go out on occasion, I often find myself experiencing this feeling of guilt. I learned that one of the best ways to avoid those feelings of guilt is by writing positive reminders to yourself in your journal, as I stated before. It's great to look back through that journal and be able to remind yourself that you are a great mom, and taking a night or a few off does not make you less of one.

Although I'm sure that we all know a few mothers who, in our opinion, probably aren't the greatest—and who do seem to be doing way more partying than being a mom, I personally don't respect that. Still, I try not to judge because you never fully know someone else's circumstances.

It's all about balance. Too much of anything could be bad. Too much mommy time with no time for self is not good, and too much partying and a small amount of mommy time definitely isn't good. That's also why it is so important to hang out with people who are like-minded, who have children as well, and who understand and respect your mommy duties and obligations.

CHAPTER 6

CO-PARENTING ISN'T EASY

Firstly, I would like to say that when you're in a relationship, before deciding to try for a baby or making careless decisions that could accidentally lead to pregnancy, be sure that you fully know and understand the character of the person you are dealing with. Do not ignore those red flags in the relationship. Do not ignore those character flaws. And definitely don't ignore the relationships they have with their prior child or children's mother(s). Pay close attention to the way they treat their other children's mothers or speak to them and about them. We'd always love to believe the person we are in a relationship with over anyone else, but if it turns out that they are the common denominator in all of their issues with the various women in their lives, nine times out of ten you will not be "the special one" who ends up not having to deal with the same sort of BS.

I definitely believe that co-parenting works much more smoothly and effectively when both parties are level-headed, mature, and internally happy with themselves. It's so unfortunate to the child involved when the parents cannot get along. These children did not ask to be placed in this world, and it's our job to be the best parents that we can be for them. This does mean keeping a healthy relationship with the other parent because it will all have some sort of effect on your child. It is important to put your pride and negative feelings to the side in co-parenting. Keep communication with the opposing parent only regarding the child you have together.

While reading *The Four Agreements*, I learned not to take anything personally. Most people act in the ways they do not because of you but simply because of who they are. If they are negative or hurtful towards you, it is only a reflection of how they are feeling inside. It is not to be taken to heart. If you have not yet read *The Four Agreements*, put that on the top of your to-do list. This book was a definite game-changer in terms of the dynamic in my relationship with my child's father. I learned that his actions, or lack thereof, truly had nothing to do with me or our child. His actions were just who he is as a person—and who he will continue to be until he works those things out with himself. It can be very frustrating when you are a full-time parent, and you are subject to dealing with a part-time parent or a when-they-feel-like-it kind of parent.

I know firsthand just how difficult it can be to co-parent with someone who you have lost most, if not all, respect for due to their lack of effort to be a good, supportive, and active parent in your child's life. When the other parent is putting forth very little effort and is willingly missing out on very important times in your child's life, such as their first birthday, this may leave you with some extremely negative feelings towards them. You may want to lash out, respond with harsh words, or fight with them. This is what I had to overcome, and I am proud to say that it is behind me. I had to decide to no longer allow this person or any person to have that kind of control over me because when you are allowing someone to anger you and disrupt your peace, you are giving them a lot of power in your life. Your child may be too young to understand this dysfunction now, but one day, they will be able to. I suggest that you do not allow it to go any further or consume any more of your energy and well-being than it already has.

I suggest praying on these issues and leaving it in God's hands. Pray to keep your peace and focus on things that you can control. Stay level-headed and just be hopeful that better days are ahead in your co-parenting efforts. Pray that the opposing parent will do what is right and what is necessary for your child sooner rather than later. Having a child tends to bring out the best or the worst in some people. I would suggest treating co-parenting like a business, and don't take things personally. I know that is easier said than done when it comes to your child, but it's so much better for everyone to maintain harmony. As long as you know that you are doing your best as a mother and your child is doing amazing regardless, just be thankful for those positives and your own strength.

CHAPTER 7

POSTPARTUM DEPRESSION IS REAL

Let's talk about postpartum depression. A study done by the Cleveland Clinic found fifty to seventy-five percent of women experience some form of PPD. I mean, think about it, ladies, we are birthing a whole human being. You are literally pushing a child out of your own body—or as in my case, you may have had a C-section. Regardless, your body is still going through so much. You created a human being, you carried that baby around for nine months, and you brought it into this world. That is a lot for one single person.

And on top of that, you may have gained weight all over; you may have experienced hair loss, acne, etc. Our bodies go through so many changes during pregnancy. Hormonal imbalances can lead to postpartum depression, and this is all completely understandable based on everything we experience. Your whole life completely changes once you bring that baby home from the hospital. Your world will no longer revolve around yourself. You have a much bigger obligation and responsibility, and you are now on mommy duty close to twenty hours out of every single day. This can become very exhausting.

It is such a blessing if you have in-house help during these early stages of your baby's life. I was so thankful to have my mom stay with me for close to two weeks when I brought Ellie home from the hospital. Her dad also came to help, and even though I did not have much respect for him at this time, as I stated earlier, you have to put your personal feelings to the side and do what is best for your child. I wanted her to be able to look back at photos and see that she did have a love of both parents surrounding her. I vowed not to allow anyone to disrupt my serenity, and that is still the mindset I exercise daily. I knew that by keeping my peace, regardless of what was going on around me or outside of me, I could reflect that same peace to my child. This was the same mindset I had during my pregnancy. I knew that whatever I felt while pregnant, she would also feel. I knew that if I were too overwhelmingly stressed, even as a fetus inside of my belly, she would feel that same stress. And I took it extremely seriously to focus on myself and my internal happiness to protect her.

When battling PPD, keep a pen and a pad next to your bed on your nightstand and write down five to ten things you are thankful for every single day. These can be as simple as being able to see, being able to use your fingers to write, or having family and friends who love and care about you. Writing these things down will realign you and put you in a state of gratitude and, I promise you, it makes the rest of your day better regardless of what you're going through or experiencing at that current moment.

Postpartum depression is real, and I do suggest that you have a strong support system and someone you can talk to about what you're experiencing. Get out of the house with your baby, go to the park or for walks in nature. Find fun hobbies to do together, and focus on just being happy—and whatever you do, don't be too hard on yourself. Work out when you can, and eat right too. Taking CBD products really helped me with PPD. The products helped to relieve stress and anxiety, and I do recommend them, but I would definitely consult with your doctor on the best options for your specific situation.

I knew I was experiencing PPD in the first few weeks of being a new mom. I would randomly cry throughout the day for no apparent reason. I no longer felt like myself, and I couldn't seem to snap out of that. I didn't want to be around anyone; I just wanted to be alone with my baby. I had extremely bad anxiety, and I was afraid to even drive in the car to her newborn doctor's appointments. I was in this state of postpartum depression, or " baby blues," for about three weeks. When I was able to get into a set routine, and I finally started getting more sleep throughout the night, I began to feel more and more like myself again, and the PPD thankfully began to fade away. I tried to write in my journal daily so that I could keep a clear timeline of what I was experiencing. This was a very helpful task to help me understand my emotions.

CHAPTER 8

BABY ESSENTIALS FOR THE FIRST YEAR

Above all, my number one recommendation would be to breastfeed your baby if you are capable. It is honestly one of the most beautiful experiences, and you will feel more connected to your baby than ever. The bonding that you receive through breastfeeding is truly amazing. Throughout my pregnancy, I began to read informative books on birth, breastfeeding, and new motherhood, and I learned so much about just how important breastfeeding can be to the health of your newborn baby.

Before reading these books, I never knew that through breast milk, your baby is literally given everything their little bodies need—every nutrient, every vitamin, literally everything. If your baby is ever sick or in need of any specific vitamin, as the mother, your body senses that and gives your baby exactly what they need through that milk. Breastfed babies are generally healthier and experience less sickness than non-breastfed babies. There are so many pros to this and no cons—not even one. All of the ignorance I used to have towards breastfeeding began to diminish. Like myself, most women worry about losing the perkiness of their breasts with breastfeeding, and yes, you definitely will, but it is all so worth it!

As moms, we will always make sacrifices. Once you have a child, there will always be someone more important than you, and you will always find yourself trying your best to do what's best for your child. As a parent, I believe we should always carry whatever burdens we have to so that our child can experience every blessing.

Unfortunately, some women cannot produce enough milk supply for their babies, and they do have to resort to formula—

and that is okay, too. Some babies are simply not able to properly latch on to the breast either. This can be very common, and I'm sure it could lead to much frustration for a ready and able mother who had plans to breastfeed. Women shouldn't be hard on themselves, feel bad about themselves, or let it bring them down if they are in this position. Formula is an amazing substitute if breast milk cannot be given. Many of us were raised on formula, and we turned out to be just fine. I solely breastfed my daughter from the day of birth until she was eight months old.

My supply began to dry up around eight months, so I implemented formula into our routine. She adjusted quite well to this, and by ten months, she was mostly formula-fed—but because of the bond that we grew through breastfeeding, she still has a strong attachment to my breasts. I also enjoy this bonding time with her. Even now, we do what I call "boob time" throughout the day whenever she has the desire. I am still slightly producing milk, but not enough to fill a bottle. It's great that she is still getting some nutrients through my breast milk even at sixteen months old, and that we are still enjoying this bonding time together.

Even if you aren't quite producing enough milk, but your baby can latch on, you can supplement what you aren't producing with formula, just like I did in the later months. If you are a mommy-to-be and the decision to breastfeed is something you are contemplating, I recommend reading up on this further and making the best decision for you and your baby.

A breast pump has to be one of the greatest inventions ever made. If you are breastfeeding, be sure to get one because nursing can really take a toll on you if you are doing it throughout the day with no pump. It can be extremely hard to get things done when you have to breastfeed your baby on a set schedule, especially if you are a busy Bad.Boss.Mom. If you pump your milk once a day, preferably in the mornings because that is when your supply tends to be the heaviest, you can refrigerate that breast milk or even freeze it and save it for later dates. Having milk stored is so helpful so that you can still get done what you need to do throughout your day, and others can help feed your baby too.

I've put together a list of the top baby items that I feel are the biggest necessities in the first year with your newborn:

- Breast pump
- Bottle sterilizer
- Baby swing
- Portable baby bed
- Baby sock monitor
- Bottle warmer
- Baby food blender
- Nooie baby cam
- Rocking chair
- Baby books
- Baby bouncer
- Wipe warmer

If you want to begin to secure your child's future while he or she is still a baby, an extremely smart move is to purchase a life insurance plan that allows your child to be the main beneficiary. Also, consider starting a savings account for your child and investing in stocks and bonds for them. We have to set our children up for financial success in their lives. I have plans to start a business for Ellie while she's young. I will make her the co-owner of that company, and I've also begun to invest and save for her monthly. When it is time, I will help to build credit for her too. I plan to teach her about the importance of financial literacy as soon as she can comprehend it all. I'll teach her how to maintain valuable assets and how to build and grow them for the rest of her life. The key is to gain financial literacy in our families forever. I plan to break my family cycle of having bad credit, no assets, not being homeowners, not owning businesses, and not being the most financially intelligent.

I am breaking that cycle currently, and I will continue to do so. I will make sure my daughter is set up for success before she leaves my home as an adult so that she can carry on the same very important values to her children, their children, and so on. Many of us in the African American community were raised with very little knowledge about the importance of all of these things. Many of us had to learn these values the hard way over time. Many of us are still trying to correct our credit, and are still trying to break these chains that have been placed on us for generations.

Thankfully I do believe we are living in times where we want to be at our best. We are striving for greatness in the African American community, and we want so much better for our children than how we were raised to be. Right now, African American women are among the top leaders in the world in terms of being new business owners and starting new businesses successfully. I believe a lot of us just have this driving force to prove the naysayers wrong, and to make a better way for our families and the generations to come. Our ancestors would be very proud!

CHAPTER 9

HOW TO HIRE A NANNY/CAN YOU AFFORD IT?

As it became more and more difficult to balance my time properly, I realized that hiring a nanny would be a complete necessity. I personally believe hiring a live-in nanny while your child is a newborn and in the early toddler stage can be much more cost-effective than the traditional daycare option. The average cost of daycare for a newborn is $300/week for the hours of 6 a.m. to 7 p.m., generally Monday to Friday. That means if you have to work in the evenings or on the weekends or simply want to get out for a little mommy time, you will still need to hire a babysitter, and that may cost you anywhere from $15 to $25 an hour. Paying for daycare and an evening or weekend sitter could end up being pretty costly.

When you have a live-in nanny, you have someone on call at all times who can usually work any hours and weekends, too, for one set weekly amount. As a serial entrepreneur with a work schedule that's not always planned, I absolutely needed someone who could be close by at all times with a very flexible schedule. A live-in nanny was perfect for my circumstances. I will break down the process of searching and hiring a live-in nanny completely for you interested moms.

Firstly, you will need to create an account with Care.com. You then need to make a post with the complete job description, detailing what exactly you are looking for in a nanny and what you are willing to pay. I listed on my job posting that I was interested in someone who could live with us because I did not have a set schedule and needed someone for different hours and times on most days. If this is a route you are interested in taking, you need to be sure you can properly accommodate your nanny. You need to be able to provide her with her own bedroom, bathroom, and groceries as part of her room and board. That's primarily how it works.

After doing some research into a fair monthly rate for the number of hours I would need my nanny each week, I created my job posting. In my posting, I offered to pay $300 weekly for a total of $1,200 monthly, free room and board, and I stated that the nanny would be required to work up to fifty hours each week. If we were to surpass those fifty hours, we would go into negotiable hourly overtime pay.

I also stated that light housekeeping and meal prep would be required with the position—although, there is never really much cleaning to do in my home because I stay pretty well on top of that. I stated that three interviews would be conducted, as well as a background check through Care.com and a thorough reference check. One interview would consist of a series of questions that I would send via text to the prospect nanny. I gave applicants fifteen minutes to get those questions answered, putting the time limit on it to ensure the questions were being answered honestly and also to get the first, most genuine answer that comes to mind.

When I put together the interview questions, I thought about what qualities were most important to me. I thought about how I planned to teach my child, what approaches I would like to be used, and what kinds of learning activities were most important to me. I thought about the kind of experience I would want the nanny to have, the kind of lifestyle the prospect nanny lives, and, very importantly, their spiritual beliefs, their level of education, and previous nanny experience. Every time I created a job posting, it would stay active for thirty days, and I would receive several applicants whose profiles I could scan through. Here is the list of interview questions that I send via text to the prospect nanny:

- How might you help my infant learn and reach milestones?
- How much experience do you have with babies?
- What would you do if my baby won't stop crying? What would you do to calm her?
- What would you do in an emergency if I wasn't in the home? (Baby choking, injury, etc.)
- What do you consider your strengths to be as a nanny?
- What are your hobbies and interests?
- What would you do to relax my baby if she won't lay down for her nap/bedtime?
- What learning activities will you do with my baby during the day while I'm away?

If I were satisfied with this first part of the interview process, I would then move forward with scheduling a FaceTime interview. During that FaceTime interview, I may ask more personal questions. You do need to get pretty personal because, after all, this is someone you will be sharing your home with. The main goals here are a happy home, a happy baby, and a positive learning environment for your child. I always ask about the prospect nanny's upbringing, core values and beliefs, dating life, spiritual beliefs, education level, and experience in the field. And, if you are anything like me—a complete OCD neat freak—you'll want to ask about their home hygiene and cleaning habits. You'll want to ask about any lifestyle habits, such as smoking, drinking, etc. At this point, I would have already run their background check through Care.com, so I would only have been moving forward with this second interview because their check was clean. It is good to obtain as much information as you can and to get a pretty good understanding of the overall person you are planning to hire. You don't want to end up with any unforeseen and unpleasant surprises later on.

It's so important that this hiring process is done thoroughly because you are trusting a complete stranger to, essentially, enter your home, become a part of your family, and take care of your most prized possession—your baby! Upon hiring the nanny, I drew up a contract through the website Rocket Lawyer. It's cheap and simple. I use a preformatted contract and make adjustments to it as needed. Listed in the contract are the job description, the requirements to be provided by me, job duties and house rules, and a few things that would lead to immediate termination, such as stealing, harming my child, etc. The contract states that, otherwise, a one-month termination notice must be given by both parties if, for any reason, things aren't working out. The nanny and I would sign the contract after going over it and agreeing to the terms and then would have it notarized.

Another very important recommendation to any moms: If you're not already doing so, I highly recommend the use of baby cameras throughout your home. This is not something I am willing to compromise on, so I advise the prospect nanny of this during the interview and make sure they are okay with being on camera while on the clock. I have a baby cam placed above my daughter's crib so I can watch her in her room, and another one in our living room and her playroom area.

Our first live-in nanny was an older woman, and she was all around pretty great. She was a mother and a grandmother herself, and she had a lot of experience. She was a great help in teaching me about many things I did not know or yet understand. I highly recommend hiring an older woman, if at all possible. I loved it—it truly felt like I had a grandmother in the house with us. She would cook quite often, and that was always really nice, too. She was with us for about three months before she, unfortunately, had to relocate to help take care of her sickly mother. So it was back to the drawing board for me. I was upset by losing her, and especially with such short notice, but I had to be understanding of her obligations to her own family that needed her. I knew Ellie, and I would miss her greatly, but it was a pleasure to have her while we did. She taught me many things in that period, and she was so vibrant and enthusiastic. She would sing and dance with Ellie nonstop.

I needed a new nanny, so right away, I reposted my job listing to Care.com and waited for prospects to apply. I would read through their profiles and check their reviews and comments on their profiles. I wasn't able to find anyone that gave me a good feeling, unfortunately. I kept checking back on the applicants for a couple of weeks, and still, no one caught my attention. After speaking to a good friend of mine from back home in Ohio about my issue, she mentioned she had a younger cousin, whom we actually went to school with, who had babysat for years and was interested in moving to Atlanta. My friend said she thought we would be a great fit for each other. I wasn't too giddy about hiring someone younger than me, because I just felt like they may not be as responsible as I would like or have the right intentions. I wanted someone who had plenty of experience, and most importantly, had a passion for it.

My friend repeatedly told me that she thought we could be a great benefit to each other and that, although her cousin was young, she was more than qualified to fill the position. Despite my better judgment, I moved forward with the three interviews, questions via text, FaceTime interview then, lastly, an in-person and final interview. I began to believe like my friend had stated that she would be a good fit for us. Unfortunately, she was not. After she moved in, I quickly concluded that her true motive was to make it down to Atlanta and gain a free place to stay with free meals. Taking proper care of my child was not at the top of her priority list. That was a very short-lived situation. She was with us for less than a month, and I then notified her I would need to look at other applicants and that she would have a month to find other living arrangements. I also offered to get her back home to Ohio.

At this point, the situation became very frustrating. I was looking for stability, most importantly. I did not want various live-in nannies in and out of my home. I knew I needed to find someone for a long-term, live-in position of at least six months to a year because I definitely knew I didn't want Ellie going to daycare until she was at least two years old. I also knew I needed to continue to work full-time so that I could be a great provider for my daughter and one day reach the level of financial freedom where I wouldn't have to trade my time for money—I learned the importance of this when reading *Rich Dad, Poor Dad*. So once again, it was back to the drawing board.

Our third nanny was a few years older than me. I hired her from Care.com, and coincidentally, we were both from Ohio. We knew mutual people, and this made me feel very comfortable. After interviewing her and loving the fact that she was a devout Christian and that we were also both Aries, I thought she would be a great fit. She was great—other than the fact that she was addicted to being on her cellphone. That was a huge problem for me. I feel like the nanny position should be treated as any other on-the-clock job—and you would lose that job very quickly if you were constantly distracted with your phone in hand. It takes two seconds for an accident to occur, or for a baby to fall, etc. Therefore, you need to focus your constant and direct attention on that child. Every time I would check in on the baby cam, the nanny had her phone in hand and face in her phone. I repeatedly expressed to her my concerns with this, and why it couldn't be tolerated. I explained that she should utilize Ellie's napping times to be on her phone. The situation did not get better, so I ultimately had to decide to let her go.

Back to the drawing board yet again! I had an applicant who stood out to me because she was bilingual. She was from Ecuador, and I thought it would be awesome if Ellie could be taught Spanish. I went through the background check and interview process, and I felt she was a great fit for us. I stated to her that I would love her to speak only in Spanish to Ellie in hopes that Ellie could pick up on this second language. Babies are like little sponges, and it is truly amazing the amount of information they obtain from everything going on all around them. This amazing bilingual nanny was with us for close to two months before she had to return to her country due to her visa expiring. That was something she failed to make me aware of until the last minute, so I was a bit frustrated with that.

Back to the drawing board *again*. I told myself, moving forward, I will only hire someone who plans to be with us for at least six months—preferably longer, but at the least six months, and I would be very firm on this during the hiring process. I learned so much about what I truly want and need in a nanny during all of these experiences with different nannies. I think that hiring a live-in nanny is a bit like dating. Everyone is perfect in the beginning, and then once they are comfortable, their true colors, intentions, and habits seem to be revealed. Sometimes issues are minor, and you can work with them and communicate through them, but this isn't always the case. Right after my daughter's first birthday, I hired my current nanny, and she has been nothing but a blessing to our life and household. It took a few learning experiences, but I feel very confident that we have found our perfect live-in nanny. She is truly a part of our little family.

I've been asked why not just use the help of family for babysitting. Unfortunately, I don't have any family living in the same state as me. I also believe that it's always best to go the professional route if you need help fulltime and if you can afford to. We all love our family and friends, but sometimes they can prove to be unreliable when continuously needed. They probably have careers of their own, too, that will need to come before them helping you with your child. If you are a hard-working mom like me, you can't afford to have unreliable childcare. It's great if you choose to rely on them for occasional help, but if you need someone who will be available daily, attentive, responsible, reliable, and treating this like a job, I recommend hiring a nanny.

When you've gone through the nanny reference check and interview, it should be clear to see that caring for children is what your nanny is passionate about. I needed someone who would be extremely passionate about taking care of my daughter and teaching her new things. Having a live-in nanny is what works best for me, and it has been just as affordable as a daycare but with many more benefits.

CHAPTER 10

IS IT OKAY TO DATE AS A NEW MOM? + DON'T GET DICKSTRACTED

Dating as a single parent can be very confusing. I feel like dating, in general, gets more and more confusing the older you get, but when a child is involved, it can be very difficult. Not only are you choosing someone for yourself, more importantly, but you're also choosing someone that you can see yourself introducing to your child at some point. And that is a major decision.

Even before I became a mom, I have never been a fan of pointless dating. I've always preferred to focus on one person that I'm really into and get serious with that one person. I've become so picky over the years that most don't even make it past phone conversations. I have a zero-tolerance checklist, and once I start checking too many boxes off in my head when speaking to someone, they don't make it much further in my world.

You can't afford to take red flags lightly when you are a single mother and dating. This is a crazy world we live in, and protecting your child should always be the first priority. So before you introduce someone to your child, you will want to spend a good amount of time thoroughly getting to know them. In my opinion, this getting-to-know period should last at least three months. It may be especially hard in the early stages of dating to know someone well or know their true intentions with you, but time definitely has a way of revealing things.

When you get to the stage of feeling comfortable with introducing this person to your child, they must understand that this is a package deal, and your child comes first. You should only be interested in someone who shows a deep interest in being there for stepping up and loving your child. Your child should be a top priority to your significant other, just as your child is a top priority to you—if you ask me, number one priority—and there should be no compromises made on any of this. Also, if you're dating someone who already has children, pay attention to how they are with their own.

If you allow something at the beginning that is not fully acceptable and fully what you want, it'll be hard to make those adjustments in the future with that same person. If you're allowing anybody in your life to get away with half-ass effort, you're setting the tone that it's okay and that it's acceptable when it is not. So always be open about how you feel, what you want, and what exactly you expect from the person you are dating. I am a force to be reckoned with! I believe that the way I carry myself keeps the BS at bay because my strong personality and strength can be very intimidating. I don't mind, because if a man is too weak to handle this, then he is not the man for me.

A relationship that many of us admire is Ciara and Russel Wilson. Russell came into Ciara's life when she was already a single mother, and he has helped to raise love and teach her son. It seems like Russell has completely taken on the role of an amazing step-parent. This is how the relationship dynamic should look when we are choosing partners as parents. Nothing less should be accepted.

In dating, before someone wins me over, I need to see that they are, first, very considerate of my mommy duties and time with my daughter and that they are not trying to distract me from that. I also have to see that they are great with kids, attentive, playful, supportive, wise, and loving.

I remember being pregnant and shocked that men were still approaching me to try to date me. I was at my favorite church one time in LA, The Potter's House, and clearly, very much pregnant, and a guy approached me and asked if I was alone. He said he noticed that I was sitting by myself most Sundays, and he then proceeded to ask if he could take me on a lunch date. I was around six months pregnant at the time. I politely declined and just couldn't believe that even with this huge baby bump, I was still being hit on by men. This went on throughout my entire pregnancy, especially on Instagram. I constantly received messages from men— even celebrities. It was quite alarming, especially when I'd be out and about and men would approach me from behind, not noticing I was pregnant, then as I turned around and they saw the bump, they would quickly apologize but still proceed to ask me out anyway or make a funny comment such as, "Well, if your husband is acting up, let me take you out sometime." I always got a good laugh out of these times but couldn't believe men just simply did not care.

Ladies, please excuse my language, but this is a term that I like to use. It sounds a bit funny, but so many of us women deal with this. I have seen almost every single one of my girlfriends throughout my life been affected by this very term, and I have fallen victim to it in the past. While on a mission to reach our goals and dreams, we must not allow ourselves to get dick-stracted.

DICK-STRACTED: Taking too much attention away from your own goals and placing it on a man, particularly because the sex is good. Good sex doesn't always equal a good partner or a good relationship.

As women, we tend to easily become distracted when we're in love or think we are in love. We tend to put our aspirations on the back burner—well, in my case, those are the mistakes I've made in my past. I believe it is key to work on yourself first. If you are already in a relationship and have a loving and supportive man, that is great. But if not, and if you have not yet reached your goals—sis, make your goals your main focus first! Once you come into complete alignment with who you are supposed to be and when you are accomplishing your goals and reaching new heights, you will attract the person who is the best for you. I believe that men also have more respect for a woman who has her shit together on her own or is working towards that.

Ladies, we can't be out here searching for our knight in shining armor if we are not the queen of our own throne. With that being said, find your purpose first. Find your own happiness, and create that happiness for yourself so that the only thing a man is doing is adding to it. I have made many mistakes in the past, mainly the type of men I was choosing to be with. I believe that comes from a deeper-rooted issue that many of us may be familiar with— "daddy issues." At the age of 26, I began to recognize the cycle I was repeating in the types of men that I was choosing to date. I didn't like what I had realized, and I have made many adjustments since then. Your decisions in life ultimately rule your life, and your future depends on these decisions. I want the best for my child and I, therefore, I needed to change my mindset and make better dating decisions right away.

Many African American households do not have a father present—it is a cycle that needs to be broken. It's also a big concern of mine and encourages me to make decisions about dating a lot more seriously. A child needs to have two parents present, whether they're biological or not. But also, ladies, please don't be so desperate to create a father figure for your child that you are just settling for anything. Being alone and at peace is much more fulfilling than being in an unhappy and unhealthy relationship. Know the difference between good sex and a good relationship. It is possible to have great sexual chemistry with someone you are not meant to be with. Do not confuse the two. Most of us women have been in a sexually pleasing relationship; some, not so much. But that one relationship, where the sex is so good that it seems like you are living in a fantasy, can either throw you off track or have you making excuses for a situation you really shouldn't even be in.

Ladies, we cannot fall victim to this. You must rise above and stay strong. I learned a little method that I practice to keep myself focused and level-headed. Come up with a list of at least five non-negotiables, and live by it! This list will display the top five most important qualities that a significant other must have to meet my standards. As soon as I realize that even one is not being met, I will not presume to be dating this person. This will help to weed out all potential BS that is not aligned with you.

Dating Non-Negotiables

My top five (and then some) are:

1. God-fearing
2. If he's a father, he must be an AMAZING ONE—no more than two children.
3. Honest and impeccable with his word
4. Motivated, ambitious, and open-minded
5. Supportive, respectful, and honest

Ladies, remember that any woman can settle. It takes an extremely strong woman to walk this road alone, to focus on herself and her goals, and to become the best version of herself for her child.

She believed she could
so she did

CONCLUSION

FIND YOUR WHY AND BOSS UP + VISION BOARD

It's so important to understand your "why," especially if you want to be a Bad.Boss.Mom. I'm sure there will be mornings you don't feel like getting out of bed and conquering the world. You're only human—you will have your days where you're just not feeling it. We all do. If you're not sure of what your why is, it may be easier to just give up. It may be easier to stay in that bed. But if you have a driving force, if you have your why and you understand your why, it will all be bigger than you.

Your why will give you that exact reason you need to keep going, keep conquering, keep overcoming obstacles, keep proving them wrong, and keep succeeding. For me, my why is my family. My father and I haven't always had the best relationship, but it has grown over the recent years. No matter what he has been through in his life, he has always shown me the meaning of resilience. I've watched him battle drug addiction, alcoholism, incarceration, and so much more. He has always bounced back from it all. He always kept his faith in God, and no matter how far he wandered away from God, he always found his way back to him. This has always motivated me to be resilient, no matter what I may have been going through. I have little sisters and brothers looking up to me, and eventually, my daughter will too, and I refuse to let any of them down. They have seen hard times that I've been through in my life, and they have applauded me through every win. They want the best for me, and they understand that with me, no one gets left behind. As soon as I reach the top, I'm throwing down that rope, and I'm pulling everyone that I love up to the top with me.

The moral of this story is Boss the F up! The only difference between you and the girl who turns into a Boss is that she took a leap of faith. She believed in something and then went after it. She trusted herself more than the idea of failing. Most of us, especially if you are an African American woman, probably didn't start at the top. Most of us start at the bottom with very little assets and work our way to the top. We have seen many strong women do this time and time again. Remember that everything that you desire is on the other side of fear. So dream big and go hard! It is so important to dream big because through the law of attraction, positive thinking, and hard work; you can literally attract any goal to yourself no matter how big it may be. So why not reach for those goals that sound crazy in your mind and your heart? Why settle for the smaller goals that seem to be more obtainable? Sometimes our mind can be our biggest enemy.

These negative thoughts kick in, override our ambitions, and try to detour us. They work against us. Often you have to be stronger than your mind. You have to keep your faith in God, and know that with him nothing is off limits!

Being a mom is all about learning the strengths you never knew you had

VISION BOARD

If you want to Boss Up, you must bring your dreams to life! At the beginning of my pregnancy, I created a vision board. I have been knocking down every goal I placed on my vision board ever since I created it. I highly recommend you create one if you haven't already. I put mine in my bedroom, on my dresser, so it's one of the first things I see when I wake up in the morning. It is a constant reminder and affirmation of my goals. I have pictures all over it of things that I am going to acquire and quotes that I aspire to live my life by.

A great saying that a friend of mine named CEO Charlie uses is that "it's already yours, time just hasn't caught up to it yet." If you start believing this in your heart, working towards it, and looking at this vision board daily, writing down your goals and positive affirmations in your journal, there is no doubt in my mind that you will acquire your heart's greatest desires! I plan on creating a new vision board to reflect my current growth and new manifestations. I plan to manifest my dream home built from the ground up, as well as vacation homes in some of my favorite places, such as Aspen Colorado, and St. Thomas. I'm manifesting an absolute abundance of health, wealth, and happiness for my family and I. I will be manifesting my multimillion-dollar business. And I will place many photos on my vision board that resonates with my goals and dreams to help other women and their families too. To get started on your vision board, here is a list of supplies you'll need:

- Cardboard poster
- Scrap magazines to take photos from

- Photos of your dream home, car, lifestyle (tip: download the Walgreens photo app and send inspo photos from your phone to be printed)
- Quotes that are meaningful to you
- Photos of your body goals
- Photos of your career goals
- Keywords that are meaningful to you, such as Yes You Can, Succeed, Happiness, Love, Dream Big!

Then, paste everything to your board, and get as creative as you'd like to be! Make it appealing to the eye and very attention-grabbing because when you're finished with it, you'll want to place it somewhere in your room or your house where you can see it every day. Recite your manifestations to yourself daily, write down your goals daily, work towards your dreams, and watch how everything begins to align for you!

Be the Girl who decided to go for it!

LETTER TO ELLIE WITH LOVE

J'elle Imani, you are truly my whole world. Since the day I found out I was pregnant with you, I began to change for the better. I began to love myself more than ever before, and I fell deeply in love with you even before meeting you. You are truly the best thing that could have ever happened to me. I carried you and cried to you and prayed to you and talked to you every day while you were in my belly. You became my best friend before you even knew it. Though my pregnancy with you wasn't easy, if I could go back in time, I wouldn't change a thing. You were the greatest reward I could have ever received for all of the struggles.

On the evening of February 10th, 2019, around 9 p.m., I began to have contractions. I was in so much pain, but I was so happy and excited because I knew I was so close to meeting you and holding your little body in my arms. Everyone was so excited to meet you. And even though your father and I had our differences, he rushed to get to the hospital to be a part of getting you here and meeting you, too. There was so much love in that hospital room awaiting your arrival. I pushed and pushed my hardest to get you here, while grandma Chrystal and your dad encouraged me to keep trying harder. Your vitals and mine were declining, so the doctor ultimately decided for an emergency C-section.

On February 11th at 6:40 p.m., you were delivered by the grace of God, my healthy and beautiful baby girl. I brought you home, and my entire world changed. I've been so much more blessed and grateful since that very day I gave birth to you. You have given me every reason to smile, even on the days that I have felt like breaking down. You have given me every reason to push through obstacles and adversities and to work harder than ever. I wrap you in my arms every day, and I thank God for you. Not one day goes by that I don't. Your scent, your cute little giggle, your feisty attitude (you get it from me), and the way you look at me and love me back makes me feel more special than anything else in this world. I'm so excited to continue this journey of life with you and to live in beautiful abundance with you.

I tell you every day how beautiful and how smart you are, and you never stop surprising me with all of the new things that you learn so quickly. I can't wait to watch you flourish. I know you will lead your life like the queen you are with the core values I am teaching you. You will love yourself and love others. You will unapologetically be whoever it is that you want to be, and I will have your back every step of your journey! I love you, my Ellie Bear, my jelly bean, my sweet baby girl, my whole world. I love you with a kind of love so deep and unconditional that you may never understand until one day you are a mother yourself. You are beautiful inside and out, you are so smart, so blessed, so protected, and you are loved beyond measure.

Love Forever,

Mommy

Do Something today
that your Future self
will thank you for

Incase no one has told you yet, I am damn proud of you Getting up, Showing up, & Never giving up!

I am a magnet for miracles and abundance

Don't call it a dream
call it a plan

Made in the USA
Monee, IL
29 August 2020

40373011R00056